Maurice Sendak

Jennifer Strand

abdopublishing.com

Published by Abdo Zoom™, PO Box 398166, Minneapolis, Minnesota 55439. Copyright © 2017 by Abdo Consulting Group, Inc. International copyrights reserved in all countries. No part of this book may be reproduced in any form without written permission from the publisher. Abdo Zoom™ is a trademark and logo of Abdo Consulting Group, Inc.

Printed in the United States of America, North Mankato, Minnesota
062016
092016

Cover Photo: Courtesy of Glyndebourne Festival Opera; Ira Nowinski/Corbis
Interior Photos: Courtesy of Glyndebourne Festival Opera; Ira Nowinski/Corbis, 1; Barbara Alper/Getty Images, 4–5; Luke Abrahams/iStockphoto, 6; Seth Poppel/Yearbook Library, 8; iStockphoto, 8–9, 10; Keystone/ Hulton Archive/Getty Images, 11; LS/AP Images, 12; Ben Gabbe/Getty Images, 13; Susan Ragan/AP Images, 14–15; AP Images, 16; myLoupe/Universal Images Group/Getty Images, 17; Richard Levine/Alamy, 18–19; James Keyser/ The LIFE Images Collection/Getty Images, 19

Editor: Emily Temple
Series Designer: Madeline Berger
Art Direction: Dorothy Toth

Publisher's Cataloging-in-Publication Data
Names: Strand, Jennifer, author.
Title: Maurice Sendak / by Jennifer Strand.
Description: Minneapolis, MN : Abdo Zoom, [2017] | Series: Amazing authors |
    Includes bibliographical references and index.
Identifiers: LCCN 2016941361 | ISBN 9781680792164 (lib. bdg.) |
    ISBN 9781680793840 (ebook) | 9781680794731 (Read-to-me ebook)
Subjects: LCSH: Sendak, Maurice--Juvenile literature. | American authors--20th
    century--Biography--Juvenile literature. | Illustrators--United States--
    Biography--Juvenile literature. | Children's stories--Authorship--Juvenile
    literature. | Authorship--Juvenile literature.
Classification: DDC 741.6/42092 [B]--dc23
LC record available at http://lccn.loc.gov/2016941361

Table of Contents

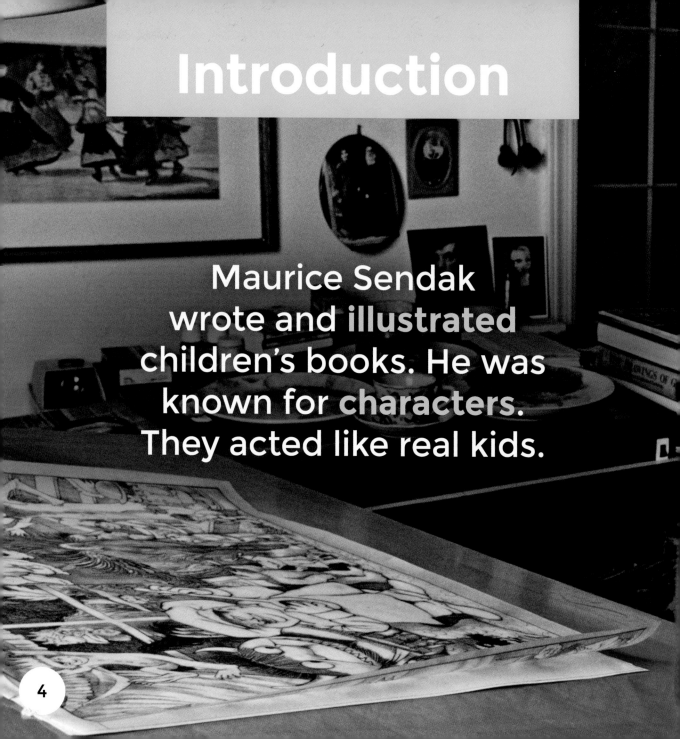

Introduction

Maurice Sendak
wrote and illustrated
children's books. He was
known for characters.
They acted like real kids.

5

Early Life

Maurice was born on
June 10, 1928.
He lived in New York.
His father told him
exciting bedtime stories.

Maurice was sick a lot.

He spent time looking
out windows.
He drew pictures
of what he saw.

Rise to Fame

Sendak became an **illustrator**.

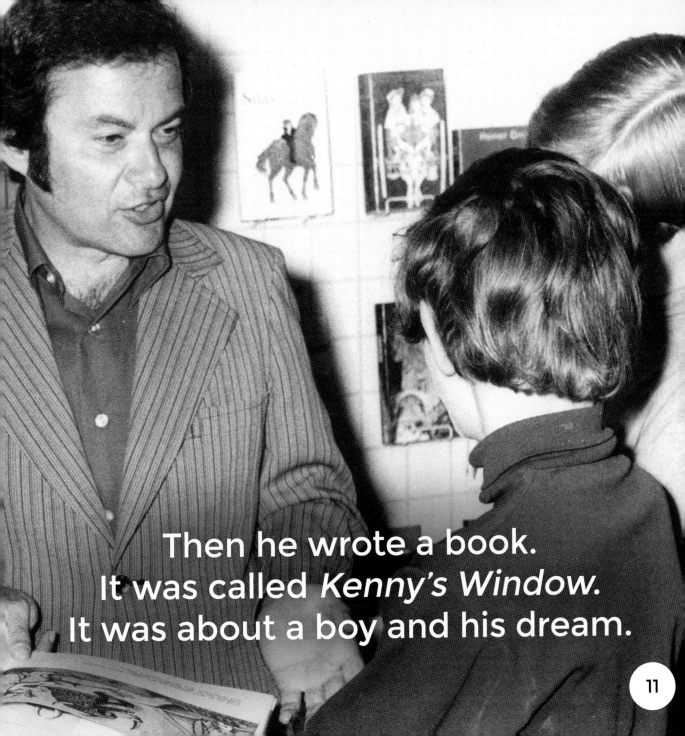

Then he wrote a book.
It was called *Kenny's Window*.
It was about a boy and his dream.

In 1963 Sendak wrote
Where the Wild Things Are.
It was about a boy
who met monsters.

The pictures were **dark**.
But the book was **popular**.

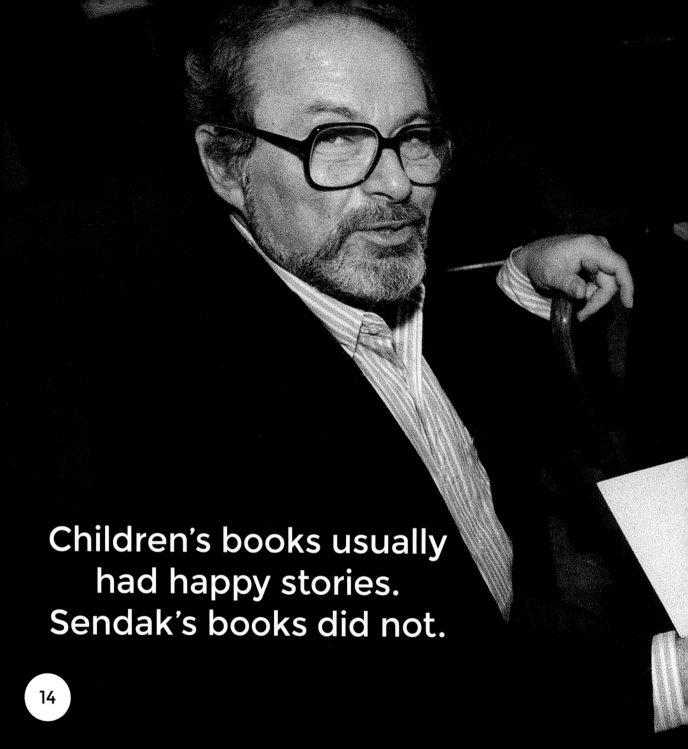

Children's books usually had happy stories. Sendak's books did not.

His characters were often angry or sad. Kids understood those feelings.

Legacy

In 1970 Sendak
won an award.

It was the Hans Christian Andersen Illustrator's Medal. This is the biggest honor for children's book illustration.

Sendak died on May 8, 2012. Some adults worried his books were too scary. But kids love them.

He is one of the world's best-known authors.

Maurice Sendak

Born: June 10, 1928

Birthplace: Brooklyn, New York

Known For: Sendak wrote and illustrated *Where the Wild Things Are.* He wrote and illustrated many other children's books.

Died: May 8, 2012

Key Dates

1928: Maurice Bernard Sendak is born on June 10.

1956: Sendak writes his first book *Kenny's Window*.

1963: Sendak's book *Where the Wild Things Are* is published.

1970: Sendak's book *In the Night Kitchen* is published.

1981: Sendak's book *Outside Over There* is published.

2012: Sendak dies on May 8.

Glossary

characters - people in a story.

dark - showing or causing bad feelings.

illustrated - added pictures to a story.

illustrator - an artist who creates pictures that help tell a story.

popular - liked or enjoyed by many people.

Booklinks

For more information
on **Maurice Sendak**, please visit
booklinks.abdopublishing.com

Z@m™ In on Biographies!

Learn even more with the Abdo Zoom
Biographies database. Check out
abdozoom.com for more information.

Index